Human Body Systems

# The Skeletal System

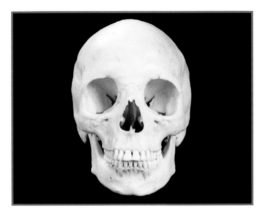

by Rebecca Olien

**Consultant:**
Marjorie Hogan, MD
Pediatrician
Hennepin County Medical Center
Minneapolis, Minnesota

Capstone
press

Mankato, Minnesota

Bridgestone Books are published by Capstone Press,
151 Good Counsel Drive, P.O. Box 669, Mankato, Minnesota 56002.
www.capstonepress.com

*Library of Congress Cataloging-in-Publication Data*
Olien, Rebecca.
    The skeletal system / by Rebecca Olien.
        p. cm.—(Bridgestone books. Human body systems)
    Summary: "Learn about the skeletal system's job, problems that may arise, and how to keep bones
healthy"—Provided by publisher.
    Includes bibliographical references and index.
    ISBN-13: 978-0-7368-5414-6 (hardcover)
    ISBN-10: 0-7368-5414-2 (hardcover)
    1. Bones—Juvenile literature. I. Title. II. Series: Bridgestone Books. Human body systems.
QP88.2.O54 2006
612.7'5—dc22                                                                                      2005021154

**Editorial Credits**
Amber Bannerman, editor; Bobbi J. Dey, designer; Kelly Garvin, photo researcher/photo editor

**Photo Credits**
Capstone Press/Gary Sundermeyer, 20; Karon Dubke, cover (girl), 4, 12 (girls), 14, 16
Photo Researchers, Inc./Alfred Pasieka/Science Photo Library, 6; Anatomical Travelogue, 12 (inset);
    Science Photo Library, 8; Science Photo Library/Alfred Pasieka, 18
Visuals Unlimited/Ralph Hutchings, cover (inset), 1, 10 (all)

012011
006038VMI

# Table of Contents

# Your Skeleton

On your mark. Get set. Go! You can run because of the bones that make up your skeleton. Bones help you bend your arms and legs. All of your bones together make up your skeletal system.

The skeletal system is just one of your body's systems. All of your body systems work together to keep you alive. You wouldn't be able to blink, burp, or bend without them.

◄ Bones work with muscles to keep you balanced in a starting position.

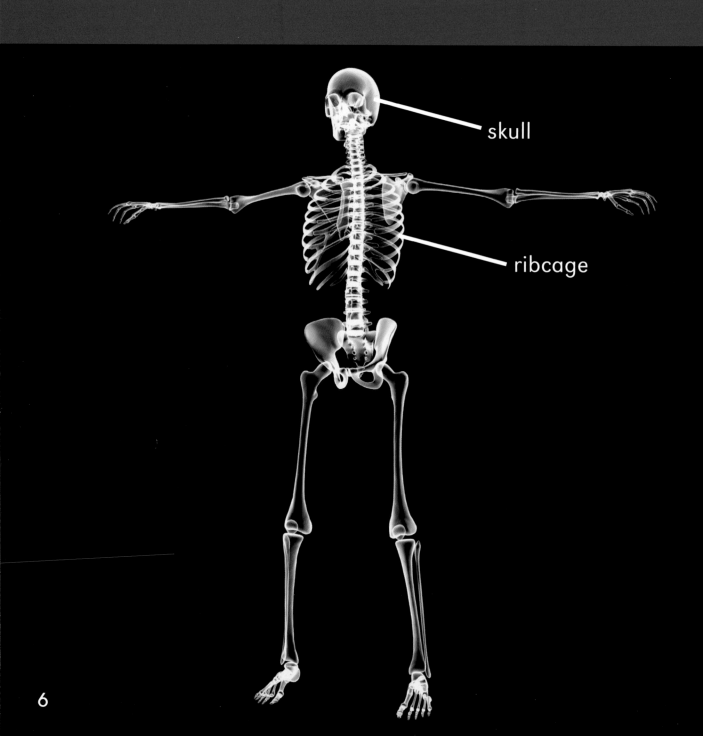

skull

ribcage

# Jobs of the Skeletal System

Your skeleton is the framework that supports your body. It gives your body its shape. Without bones, you'd be a saggy bag of skin!

The skeleton protects **organs**. The ribcage protects your heart, lungs, and liver from injury. The skull acts like a natural helmet to protect your brain when you bump your head.

Bones have other important jobs. They store **calcium** and other minerals our bodies need. Almost all the blood in our bodies is made inside bones.

◄ Bones stack on top of one another to hold the body upright.

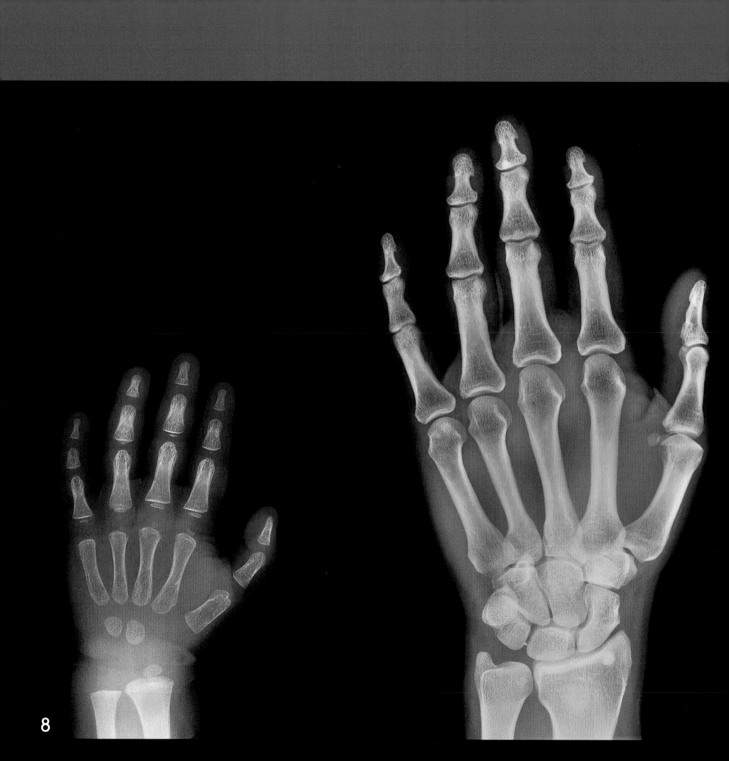

# Bones

Bones have two parts. The outside of a bone is made of hard calcium and other minerals. Calcium makes bones strong. Inside the bone is a spongy material called **marrow**. Blood cells are made in bone marrow.

Children's bones **fuse** together, growing longer and stronger each year. When you were born, you had about 300 bones. By the time you're an adult, you'll have about 206 bones.

◄ The bones in the 3-year-old's hand (left) haven't all grown together yet. All the gaps between the bones in the adult's hand (right) have closed.

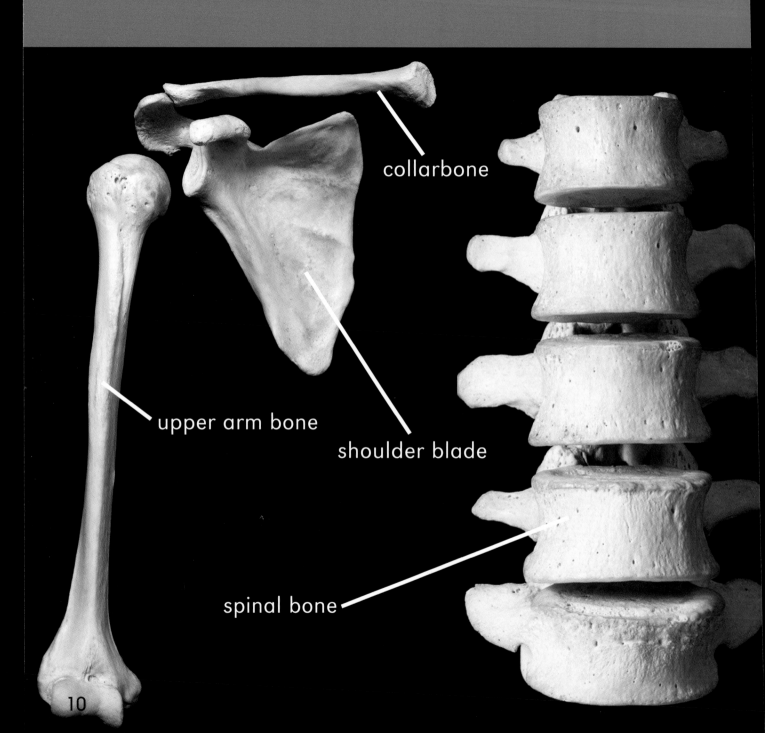

collarbone

upper arm bone

shoulder blade

spinal bone

# Size and Shape of Bones

Three main kinds of bones make up the human skeleton. Long bones, like the upper arm bone, are found in arms and legs. The collarbone is a long bone that supports the weight of the whole arm. Short, blocky bones allow you to bend. These bones are found in your spine, feet, ankles, hands, and wrists. Curved bones form the shoulders, pelvis, ribs, and skull.

◄ Skeletal bones have three different shapes.

elbow

# Joints

Your elbow is a hinge and pivot **joint**. It connects bones in the upper and lower arm. Hinge joints make your arms move back and forth like a door. Pivot joints help you rotate and twist your arms.

Your ball-and-socket joints move you the most. These joints are in hips and shoulders. Ball-and-socket joints allow legs and arms to move in circles. Dancers and gymnasts use these joints a lot.

◄Joints let your arm bones move in an arm wrestling match.

# How Bones Work

To move your body, you use many bones at the same time. The whole skeleton supports and moves a soccer player. Long bones in the leg move the body forward. The knee joint allows the leg to bend. Foot bones turn at the ankle joint. The player kicks the ball with the bones in the foot.

◄ Your longest and strongest bones are in your legs.

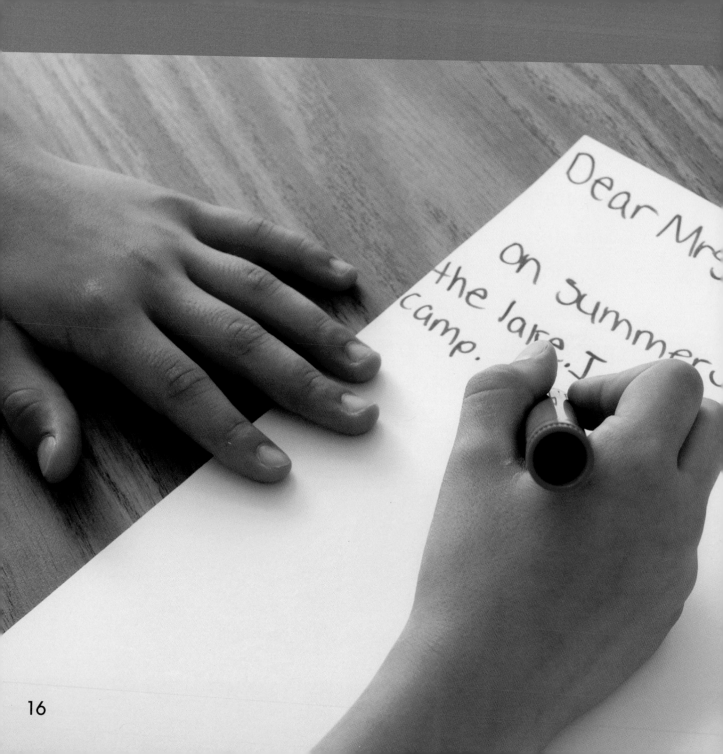

# Bones and Muscles

Muscles move bones into action. Strong cords called **tendons** connect muscles to bones. Muscles pull on tendons, which pull on bones.

Muscles squeeze to pull a bone forward. You can write because muscles move the bones in your hands. To walk, muscles pull on leg bones. Muscles even move your ribs when you breathe.

◄ Each thumb has two bones. The rest of your fingers have three bones each.

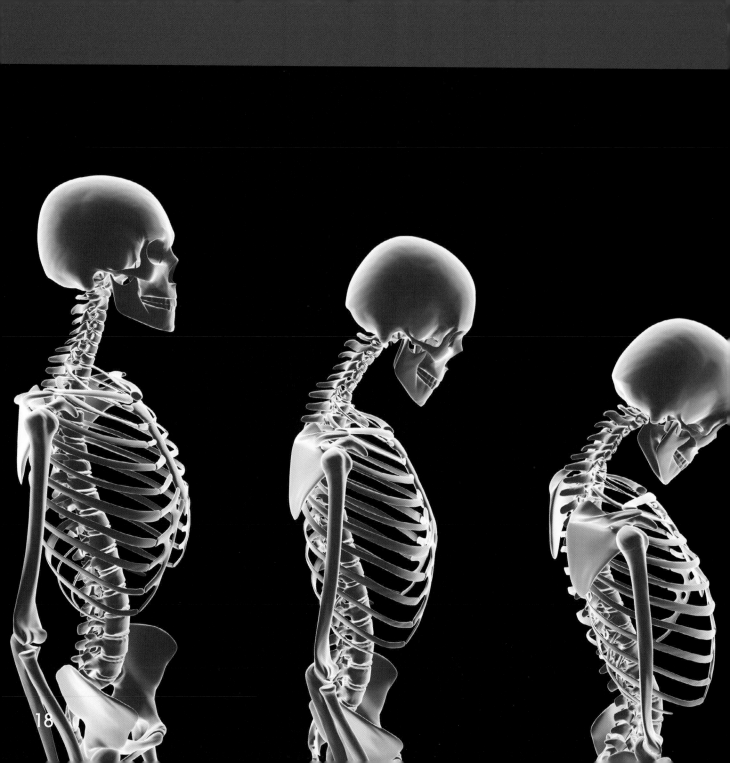

# Problems with Bones

Bones are strong, but they can break. Broken bones start to heal themselves right away with swelling. Blood rushes to the area of the break. In about one to two weeks, soft rubbery **callus** starts to fill in the cracked bone. This callus continues to fill for several months. Stronger bone slowly replaces callus until the bone is mended.

**Osteoporosis** is a disease millions of adults get as they age. It causes bones to lose calcium and to become thinner. Thin bones are weak and can break easily.

◄ When someone gets osteoporosis, their normal spine (far left) changes into a hunched, curved one (far right).

# Keeping Bones Healthy

Exercise and good nutrition keep bones healthy. Exercising makes bones thicker and stronger. Bones need calcium, a mineral found in dairy foods. Milk, cheese, and ice cream all have calcium. Bones also need vitamin D. Vitamin D is found in foods like fish and eggs. Sunlight helps your body take in vitamin D.

Wearing safety gear protects your bones when rollerblading. A hard plastic helmet protects the skull. Knee and elbow pads cushion joints. Taking care of your bones will keep you healthy and strong.

◄ Milk helps bones and teeth grow strong.

# Glossary

calcium (KAL-see-uhm)—a soft, silver-white mineral found in teeth and bones; milk is a good source of calcium.

callus (KA-luhs)—a mass of tissue that forms around a broken bone

fuse (FYOOZ)—to join together; bones fuse together.

joint (JOINT)—a place where two bones meet; knees, elbows, and hips are joints.

marrow (MAR-oh)—the soft substance inside bones that is used to make blood cells

organ (OR-guhn)—a part of the body that does a job; the heart and lungs are organs.

osteoporosis (ahs-tee-oh-puh-ROH-sis)—a disease where bones become brittle from calcium loss

tendon (TEN-duhn)—a strong cord of tissue that connects a muscle to a bone

# Read More

**DeGezelle, Terri.** *Your Bones.* The Bridgestone Science Library. Mankato, Minn.: Bridgestone Books, 2002.

**Parker, Steve.** *Skeleton.* DK Eyewitness Books. New York: DK Publishing, 2004.

# Internet Sites

FactHound offers a safe, fun way to find Internet sites related to this book. All of the sites on FactHound have been researched by our staff.

Here's how:

1. Visit *www.facthound.com*
2. Type in this special code **0736854142** for age-appropriate sites. Or enter a search word related to this book for a more general search.
3. Click on the **Fetch It** button.

# Index